PATHFINDER WAS BORN WITH THE OCTOBER REVOLUTION

Mary-Alice Waters

PATHFINDER
NEW YORK LONDON MONTREAL SYDNEY

COVER ILLUSTRATION: Patrick Heron, *Rumbold Vertical I: Emerald in Reds:* February 1970. © 2000 Artists Rights Society (ARS), New York / DACS, London

COVER DESIGN: Eric Simpson

ISBN 978-0-87348-922-5
Library of Congress Control Number 2009930817

Manufactured in Canada

First edition, 2000
Sixth printing, 2024

PATHFINDER
www.pathfinderpress.com
Email: pathfinder@pathfinderpress.com

Pathfinder was born with the October Revolution

BY MARY-ALICE WATERS

FIRST OF ALL, a thank you to Casa Editora Abril for taking the initiative to organize this conference as part of the events surrounding the Eighth International Book Fair that opens here in Havana tomorrow. It gives us all a rare opportunity to share experiences and discuss how to do a more effective job in meeting those goals we hold in common.

Pathfinder Press was born with the October Revolution. As a publishing house, our direct line of continuity goes back to the earliest publication in the United States of speeches and writings by Lenin, on the eve of the 1917 revolutions

---

A conference on Political and Social Publishing in the 1990s took place in Havana, Cuba, February 2–3, 1998, sponsored by Casa Editora Abril, publishing house of the Union of Young Communists (UJC). Mary-Alice Waters, president of Pathfinder Press, and a member of the National Committee of the Socialist Workers Party, was among the speakers who addressed the meeting. This article was originally published in the *Militant*, February 16, 1998.

in Russia. That is when magazines like the *International Socialist Review*, produced in the United States by left-wing militants in the Socialist Party, began publishing articles by the Bolshevik leader.

Origins in 1919

Following the victorious October 1917 insurrection of the workers, peasants, and soldiers of the tsarist empire, which opened the road to the first socialist revolution, revolutionary-minded working people the world over sought to understand and follow the example of the first worker-bolsheviks. By 1919 a regroupment of left-wing Socialists, members of the Industrial Workers of the World, and others had come together in the United States to found something truly new—the communist movement in North America, whose explicit goal was to emulate the Bolsheviks. Through many and varied channels they began to publish the periodicals, pamphlets, and books that for the first time in the twentieth century brought to the working class in our hemisphere a communist perspective that drew on the toilers' initial experience of taking power, defending it, and using it worldwide.

I start with this because it is the clearest way I can explain what guides the editorial policy of Pathfinder to this day. For more than eighty years, Pathfinder and its various predecessors (from Merit and Pioneer, all the way back to the Literature Department of the Workers Party of America) have had one and only one objective: to publish and distribute as widely as possible the books, pamphlets, and magazines that are necessary to advance the construction of a communist party in the United States—an objective inseparable from the building of a communist movement internationally.

From 1917 to today, we have sought to defend a course true to Lenin's leadership of the Russian Revolution and the early years of the Communist International. Lenin's political trajectory was the opposite of the course that later became identified with the Stalin-led Communist Party of the Soviet Union—the consequences of which are being registered in the colossal events of recent years that continue to unfold throughout Central Europe, the Balkans, and the former Soviet republics. Pathfinder has always prioritized printing works created by revolutionists who exemplified Lenin's internationalist and proletarian course in deeds as well as words.

We begin with the world and the ongoing facts before us, with the most important challenges of the world class struggle, thinking about how to strengthen the fighting vanguard of the working class so it is better armed to understand the world in which we live; to understand the history of the modern working-class movement; to become more conscious of its strength and historic responsibilities; and to chart a line of march toward taking power in order to open the road to the construction of socialism.

Communism: a movement, not a doctrine

We have always subscribed to Engels's famous response to Karl Heinzen, written in 1847 a few months before Karl Marx and Frederick Engels drafted the founding document of the modern workers movement, the *Communist Manifesto*. "Communism is not a doctrine, but a movement," Engels wrote. "It proceeds not from principles but from facts. Insofar as it is a theory, [it] is the theoretical expression of the position of the proletariat" in its struggle with the bourgeoisie and the "theoretical summation of the conditions for the liberation of the proletariat" and its allies from exploitation and oppression.

To bring this home for us today, I want to use the example of one of the most important books that Pathfinder has published in the last eight years. It is entitled *U.S. Hands Off the Mideast! Cuba Speaks Out at the United Nations*. It was published in English and Spanish in October 1990 as Washington was driving toward the brutal, massive assault on Iraq that began in January 1991. Cuba's then-ambassador to the United Nations, Ricardo Alarcón, speaking from the seat Cuba fortuitously held on the Security Council, was the only voice speaking out clearly and consistently, utilizing the arena of international diplomacy, against the imperialist war being mounted under the auspices of the United Nations flag.

Pathfinder, in a matter of days (literally) brought out a small booklet containing each and every one of Alarcón's speeches to the world, along with the main speech by Fidel condemning Washington's aggression. When that sold out in a few weeks, we printed a second, expanded edition, so that communists and anti-imperialist fighters around the world could use it to campaign against the war that the magazine *New International* rightly calls "the opening guns of World War III."

In the short space of six months, Pathfinder sold some 10,000 copies of that title in English, and 1,500 in Spanish.

Today, as Washington is again accelerating toward a new murderous—and cowardly—assault on the people of Iraq, that Pathfinder title takes on renewed importance.[1]

1. In February 1998, Washington and its imperialist allies were threatening widespread air strikes against Iraq on the pretext that Baghdad

The fact that—as is our policy—we have not allowed the book to go out of print means that our weapons are ready, and, as we meet here, it is again being used by opponents of Washington's course around the world.

In a similar way, thirty years ago Pathfinder published another book—*Che Guevara Speaks*. In December 1967, only weeks after the death in combat of Ernesto Che Guevara, while news of his brutal murder by CIA-trained forces of the Bolivian military dictatorship and the implications of that event still resounded like a drumbeat around the world, Pathfinder published the first edition of that collection of speeches and writings. We have not allowed it to go out of print from that day to this.

Briefly, I would like to enumerate some of the facts and policies that guide our publishing efforts. I hope they will provoke some discussion and comment.

1. Pathfinder is not formally or legally the publishing house of a political party (it has its own corporate structure and lines of decision making). At the same time, from the beginning the writers, editors, directors, and production personnel have all been active communist cadres in the

was refusing to allow "arms inspectors" unlimited access to whatever site they demanded, in continued violation of the country's sovereignty. In December 1998 this culminated in four days of murderous air strikes throughout Iraq conducted by United States and United Kingdom forces. Between early 1997 and November 2000, some 16,000 sorties launched more than 1,000 bombs and missiles against more than 250 targets in northern Iraq. Over 300 people, mostly civilians, were killed in these raids, according to Iraqi estimates.

United States (communists with a small 'c'), experienced in the working-class movement. Pathfinder is the publishing house that has always kept in print the major documents, resolutions, and speeches of leaders of the Socialist Workers Party. In the historical perspective, this is one of its most important and irreplaceable accomplishments. Without this, the documents that both reflect and guide the practical work of communist workers, students, and their allies in the United States would be nowhere available.

The Changing Face of U.S. Politics: Working-Class Politics and the Trade Unions by SWP national secretary Jack Barnes—a new edition of which has been published by Pathfinder in three languages (English, Spanish, and French)—is the most recent important example of this central core of our publishing.

Produced in heat of political battles

2. As has been true throughout the history of the workers movement, the best materials we publish are almost without exception those produced by revolutionists in the heat of political battle—not abstract analyses or distanced studies, but pamphlets and books written by those who are responding to the needs of the day.

One of the best examples of this is a book written in the anti-Nazi underground during World War II by a young Belgian, who was a Jew. *The Jewish Question*, by Abram Leon, perhaps the finest historical materialist study of this question ever to be written, was put down on paper while Leon was active in the underground. He finished it only a short time before he was captured and died at the hands of the Gestapo. Sailors, merchant marine men who were members of the SWP and often acted as couriers internationally, were able to salvage a copy of the manuscript in the closing days of the war. Pathfinder translated it, published it, and has kept it in print for decades.

Since 1928 when the *Militant* first began publishing—and 1931 when Pathfinder's predecessor Pioneer Publishers produced its first title—there has always been a close working collaboration between the newspaper and the publishing house. Many of the materials that eventually find their way into Pathfinder publications first appear in the pages of the *Militant*. It couldn't be otherwise with a publishing house that is always in the thick of struggles and seeking to promote a clear class perspective.

From the beginning of the Cuban Revolution, for example, the *Militant* has been the main periodical in the United States that published important documents and speeches by leaders of the Cuban Revolution. These were often then rapidly reprinted by Pioneer Publishers as pamphlets and used widely by the active defenders of the Cuban Revolution both in the United States and Canada, many of whom organized themselves during the revolution's opening years as the Fair Play for Cuba Committee.

In the days before photo-offset printing, it was especially important to be able to reuse the hot-lead type set for the newspaper, which was by far the costliest element in the printing process.

Pamphlets such as *The Second Declaration of Havana* were first published this way, for example—another title that Pathfinder has kept continuously in print, in this case since 1962. Tomorrow, in fact—February 4—we will be marking the 36th anniversary of that call to action to the toilers of the Americas. We still use it widely as one of the best and most basic pieces of literature we have to explain the character of U.S. imperialist domination of Latin America, the inevitable resistance to it, and the place of the Cuban Revolution in that uncompromising resistance.

Just in the last days, the most recent example of this kind of collaboration came off the press, in English and Spanish. *Celebrating the Homecoming of Ernesto Che Guevara's Reinforcement Brigade to Cuba*. It is a collection of articles published in the *Militant* last year, including a series of articles, interviews, and speeches about Che by those who knew and worked with him as a leader of the Cuban Revolution, a number of them reprinted from various publications here in Cuba. It also includes an excellent piece by Algerian revolutionary leader Ahmed Ben Bella, reprinted from *Le Monde diplomatique*.

The bulletin format of this title allows for rapid, and relatively less expensive, publication of materials that might not otherwise be quickly available and easily accessible. Over the years, a number of publications like this have eventually evolved into Pathfinder books.

What is needed, not what is profitable

3. Pathfinder's starting point has always been what is needed by those fighting to change the world, not what will sell in the marketplace. In other words, what guides us is the opposite of what guides any bourgeois publishing house. Moreover, with limited resources, we have always had to choose carefully, and often had to make painful decisions, on what, and what not, to publish. We do well to publish four or five new titles in a year's time, although in 1997 we were able to bring out twelve new titles, including five in Spanish and four in French. That's exceptional.

Our guideline, and this is especially true of books, is to

publish materials that have a lasting value, that deal—in something more than a conjunctural way—with questions that are and will remain central to the working-class movement for years.

For us—and again this is the opposite of any capitalist business—what is important is what publishers call their "backlist." We keep in print the titles that contain the crystallized work of decades—upgrading and improving their presentation when possible, but keeping them in print in any case. That in-print backlist gives us great leverage, allowing a relatively small cadre of communists to have substantially more weight than would otherwise be possible.

In the last year alone we have reprinted eighty-three of our titles as we strive to approach capitalist norms of efficiency and stock control with small runs and just-in-time delivery. That is an enormous challenge that we don't always meet.

Some books, like *Lenin's Final Fight*, published last year in Spanish for the first time, are actually titles Pathfinder has had in print for seventy years or more, in one or another edition or collection.

All told, Pathfinder has more than 330 titles in print today. Some 280 are in English, 31 in Spanish, 16 in French, and a number in Russian. Together with Pathfinder supporters and collaborators in other countries, several Pathfinder titles are also published in Swedish, Farsi, Greek, and Icelandic.[2]

2. Between early 1998, when this talk was given, and late 2000, Pathfinder, including the magazine *New International*, published twenty-three new titles—thirteen in English, six in Spanish, three in French and one in Swedish.

4. Most of the books we print, of course, are works that no one else is interested in publishing, because there is no other English-language publisher that shares Pathfinder's objectives.

Books like *Fighting Racism in World War II*, for example, which tells the story of the fight against segregation and discrimination in the U.S. armed forces, war industries, and elsewhere, even as the Second World War was unfolding. Or the magnificent series of books Pathfinder has published on the documents of the early years of the Communist International. These were things we had no competition for.

The same can be said for some of the books that are today among our best-sellers—speeches by Malcolm X. Malcolm was one of the most outstanding leaders of the working class in the United States in the twentieth century, a man who was killed by his enemies precisely because of his uncompromising revolutionary and internationalist trajectory and his contempt for anything but the truth. At the time Pathfinder began publishing Malcolm—while he was still alive—many on the left in the United States were denouncing him as a racist, and even a fascist. Fidel and Che, who were warmly welcomed to Harlem by Malcolm, understood his magnificent leadership qualities the same way we did.

In the words of revolutionists

Pathfinder always tries to publish books by revolutionary leaders, letting them speak for themselves in their own words. I would say we give precedence to such books over works by others about the great revolutionary leaders and events of our epoch. Workers, revolutionary-minded young people, don't primarily need interpreters, explainers, intermediaries. They can do the work of reading and studying for themselves and over time understand more and more, especially if they discuss what they are reading with fellow fighters. They gain self-confidence by knowing that they can read Marx, or Lenin, or Malcolm, or Che, and by working together to understand more deeply what such kindred spirits are talking about.

Pathfinder's "Speaks" series is one that captures this well: *Rosa Luxemburg Speaks, Leon Trotsky Speaks, Malcolm X Speaks, Che Guevara Speaks, Sandinistas Speak, Nelson Mandela Speaks, Thomas Sankara Speaks, Maurice Bishop Speaks, W.E.B. Du Bois Speaks, Eugene V. Debs Speaks.*

That is why we publish books of speeches and writings by leaders of the Cuban Revolution—by Ernesto Che Guevara and by Fidel Castro especially. To let the Cuban Revolution speak for itself, through its most capable representatives.

And today, with the writings of Marx, Engels, and Lenin—previously readily available from the publishing houses of the Soviet Union—becoming more and more difficult to obtain, we anticipate that Pathfinder will of necessity have to face the responsibility to somehow fill that gap as well.

Bearers of culture

5. At the point where politics and broader questions of culture intersect, the working-class movement constantly wages battle against both bourgeois dominance and mind-deadening escapism. From Marx and Engels to Che and Fidel, the great working-class leaders of our epoch have always fought to make the highest cultural conquests within class

society the property of working people. They have done so knowing that it is working people who will be not only the bearers of the best of bourgeois culture into the new society, but will be among the great majority who more and more become the confident creators of culture.

Pathfinder considers the publication of works such as *Art and Revolution* by Leon Trotsky (with its trenchant polemic against the Stalin bureaucracy's politics of socialist realism), *What is Surrealism?* by André Breton, and one of our newest titles, *John Coltrane and the Jazz Revolution of the 1960s* by Frank Kofsky, to be a necessary part of our publishing program. As Malcolm X insisted, broadening your scope makes working people better, and more effective, political people. It also enables them to fight with more joy.

For the same reason we are proud to help distribute internationally *La Gaceta de Cuba*, published by the Union of Writers and Artists of Cuba, as we do *Granma* and *Cuba Socialista*, published by the Communist Party of Cuba.

Depend on volunteer labor

6. Pathfinder is only able to maintain this kind of publishing program because of the generous support of communist-minded workers around the world. They subsidize our publishing program because they agree with it, and they make real sacrifices to keep these revolutionary weapons in print. Pathfinder loses money on every book it publishes. It has never had a year, or even a quarter, when it broke even.

The economics of publishing quality books in small runs means that even with such subsidies Pathfinder books are expensive for working people. For this reason, several years ago we set up the Pathfinder Readers Club to make our books accessible to more readers. For $10 per year anyone can join the club, and receive all Pathfinder titles at 15 percent off the cover price at any Pathfinder bookstore, or by ordering directly. And throughout the year we offer even higher discounts on selected titles.

We also depend on volunteer labor by Pathfinder's supporters to translate, copyedit, proofread, scan and format, set type, design covers—some of which are truly beautiful—and do all the other time-consuming work that is necessary to produce and distribute printed materials.

In fact, we have just begun what will surely be one of our most ambitious endeavors ever, all with volunteer labor. Some two hundred Pathfinder supporters from almost a dozen countries around the world, are preparing every single title currently in print by Pathfinder in digital form. Every book and pamphlet is being scanned, proofread and formatted, and often indexed. Every cover and photo signature is being reconstructed in digital files. Thanks to this enormous effort, which will take several years to complete, Pathfinder will be able to continue to take advantage of advances in computer-to-plate printing technology. We will be able to print small quantities, reprint frequently as demand requires, and continue to upgrade new editions as our resources permit.

Every title will be ready-to-print as needed. And we will also be able to develop a Pathfinder website to make the fruits of this effort accessible around the world. Without the volunteer labor of our supporters around the world, none of this would be possible.

Volunteers are also now finishing the work to produce a series of three CD-ROMs that will contain the entire collection of almost sixty-five years of the journal of Marxist theory and politics, *New International*. With only a few copies of many of the early years of the magazine in existence, we were in danger of losing this irreplaceable resource entirely. Now it will once again be readily available to new generations of communists in the U.S. and around the world.

7. The sale and distribution of Pathfinder titles also depends on the volunteer efforts of supporters. First and foremost, Pathfinder sales are "street sales"—sales by communist youth and workers off folding card tables set up regularly on street corners in workers districts, at plant gates, on university campuses, near high schools, at political events, wherever workers and young people capable of being attracted toward revolutionary politics may gather.

An international network of Pathfinder bookstores in seven countries is another important source of sales. These also are organized completely by volunteers, by workers and students who organize to keep the stores open as many hours a week as possible.

The same volunteers also act as sales representatives, visiting regular commercial bookstores, libraries, and professors in dozens and dozens of cities, discussing the books with buyers and teachers. They obtain orders that are placed either directly with Pathfinder or through wholesale distribution businesses that buy from Pathfinder as well as other publishers.

Through these kinds of volunteer efforts—which include taking Pathfinder booths to numerous international book fairs around the world, from Moscow to Frankfurt, from Tehran to Göteborg, from Guadalajara to Sydney to Havana—the reach of our publication effort is truly surprising.

8. A special word about our publishing in Spanish. Our

Spanish-language publishing began, in a modest way, in the 1930s as the communist movement in the United States increased its collaboration with revolutionary fighters in Mexico, Puerto Rico, Cuba, and the Dominican Republic. A not insignificant part of this, again, was due to the efforts of communists who were part of the merchant marine, who frequently sailed to the major ports of the Caribbean.

Chicano fight propels Spanish titles

But the modern period of publishing in Spanish owes its impetus to the new rise of the Chicano movement in the United States at the end of the 1960s—part of the revolutionary upsurge throughout Latin America in the wake of the 1959 victory in Cuba and the defeat of U.S. imperialism at the Bay of Pigs. The upsurge of the Chicano movement was also the product of the growing mass opposition within the United States to Washington's aggression against the people of Vietnam, and the determination of young Chicanos to do everything possible to end that war—a war in which they were being conscripted to fight and die, waged against a people for whom they had nothing but growing respect. The powerful example of the struggle for Black liberation, followed by the rising wave of struggles by women against their oppression, were a mighty impetus to the Chicano movement, as well.

That is when *Perspectiva Mundial*, the Spanish-language sister publication of the *Militant,* was born. As with the *Militant* earlier, collaboration between *PM* and Pathfinder has been the source of a growing arsenal of books and pamphlets in Spanish.

Pathfinder's first book in Spanish was published in 1981. That was *Wall Street enjuicia al socialismo*—the court record of the trial and conviction on subversion charges of the entire central leadership of the SWP and leaders of the Midwest Teamsters union on the very eve of World War II (in fact they were sentenced to prison the day after Pearl Harbor). Published in English as *Socialism on Trial*, it contains the actual court testimony of James P. Cannon, a founding leader of the communist movement in the United States and of the Socialist Workers Party. This is a book we have used in English and Spanish for decades as a very basic piece of communist education and propaganda. It is similar in this regard to Fidel's 1953 courtroom speech, "History Will Absolve Me," though, needless to say, it did not have the historical impact of that document. That day will come!

With the major increase in immigration to the United States from throughout Latin America in the last decades—a wave of immigration that is similar in size and historic weight to the immigration from Europe at the end of the last century—the need for a growing arsenal of weapons in Spanish has increased even more. It is not only Los Angeles, Houston, and Miami that are today major Spanish-speaking metropolitan centers. The composition of the working class within the U.S. has changed dramatically from coast to coast, even in small towns and in every basic industry.

The working class has been strengthened by this influx of working people from throughout Our America, who are every day more and more confident about their ability to be active vanguard fighters in class-struggle battles within the United States. A communist party in the United States today is inconceivable without a strong component of Spanish-speaking members within its leading cadres, a cadre that reflects the working class as it is, and as it is becoming. Nor is it conceivable without a strong publishing program in Spanish.

Even though I won't take time to expand on the point here, it is important to note that our French-language publishing program, a product of collaboration between Pathfinder and communists in Canada, is born out of similar necessities dictated by the class struggle in North America, and the powerful new rise of the independence movement in Quebec, beginning in the 1960s.

In addition to its own titles in Spanish, Pathfinder distributes dozens more of the classics of Marxism as well as many titles imported from publishers in Cuba. This year, for the first time ever, we received substantial volunteer help from a team of comrades in Cuba, at the University of Matanzas, whose efforts made possible the publication of *La última lucha de Lenin* [Lenin's final fight], in an edition that includes corrected and improved Spanish translations of Lenin's final writings, all of which were checked against the Russian original by comrades who had studied for years in the Soviet Union.

9. Several times I have mentioned the magazine *New International*. Like many publishing houses associated with the communist movement, Pathfinder helps to promote and distribute a political and theoretical magazine that has its own imprint. Editora Política, for example, the publishing house of the Central Committee of the Communist Party of Cuba, helps to produce and distribute *Cuba Socialista*. *New International*, as the magazine we distribute is now known (like Pathfinder it has had several different names over the decades since it first began publishing in 1934), is published in English and translated into three other languages—Spanish, French, and Swedish. It plays

an indispensable role in our overall arsenal, focusing as it does on the most important questions of world politics and presenting a communist line in practice on the burning issues of today.

Exacting and demanding standards

10. Before closing with a few words about our work publishing titles that spread the truth about the Cuban Revolution, I want to address one other point.

For us, the care with which we edit and prepare every single book or pamphlet we produce is the most important test of our publishing efforts. We consider this to be a class question. If it is to prepare itself to be the ruling class, the working class must have access to truth, to culture, to clearly presented, accurate information. Their own history and continuity must be made accessible to new generations of fighters as they enter the struggle. These are things that Che understood and fought for so well. The working class must learn to be exacting in the standards of quality it demands in all things. That is one of the sources of our self-respect and self-confidence. Those who belong to the class that produces everything know better than anyone when work is done with care and when it is shoddy and unworthy of their efforts.

A publishing house that strives above all to provide revolutionary fighters with access to the world class struggle that they must know about and understand in order to be effective in transforming themselves and that world—a publishing house with such a goal must maintain the highest possible standards of accuracy.

A misspelled name; an incorrect date; an erroneous or confusing or even uncomfortable translation; an inaccurate footnote or caption (or none at all where one is needed for the new young reader or the worker or farmer for whom reading is still a challenge); lack of care in presenting pictures, maps, or other aids to the reader; covers that are ugly or lack inspiration and work; printing that is too light and unreadable; type that is so small it discourages the reader; a book that is carelessly bound or cut—all these are lapses that pain us when they occur. And they should. They are not worthy of the working class and its historic tasks.

None of these flow from problems created by the limits on material resources from which we all suffer one way or another. They are questions of political training and discipline and respect for our class. They exemplify proletarian habits, which are the wellspring of discipline.

At root, these are the same questions that were at the center of the deliberations and decisions of the Fifth Congress of the Communist Party of Cuba when it convened a few months ago, in October 1997: the revolution, the working class, has to prove it can be *more* efficient, and produce with *greater* quality than the capitalists. And it can.

Seventy titles on Cuban Revolution

11. Out of the 351 books and pamphlets and *New Internationals* that Pathfinder is responsible for keeping in print, 70 are directly related to the Cuban Revolution. Four full pages of the 1998 Pathfinder catalog are devoted to titles on "The Cuban Revolution in world politics." Everything from six volumes of speeches by Cuban president Fidel Castro, to *Socialism and Man in Cuba*, to *Women and the Cuban Revolution*, to *How Far We Slaves Have Come!* by Fidel and Nelson Mandela, to *Dynamics of the Cuban Revolution*

by the late SWP leader Joseph Hansen—in addition to the three titles singled out yesterday by Iraida Aguirrechu of Editora Política that have been published in the last few years, working together with that publisher. The *Bolivian Diary of Ernesto Che Guevara*, Che's *Episodes of the Cuban Revolutionary War*, and *Pombo: A Man of Che's 'guerrilla'* by Harry Villegas, are books that would not have been possible in their current form or with the quality they attained without the aid of Editora Política. For us, such collaboration is priceless.

The significant number of titles published by Pathfinder that aim to present the truth about the Cuban Revolution is, I believe, a vivid concretization of the importance of the Cuban Revolution in today's world, its actual weight in the world class struggle. Because Pathfinder has never set out to be a publisher of books about Cuba. To the contrary, we have always tried to bring the Cuban Revolution into sharp focus as part of the world, and part of history.

Publishing books and pamphlets about the Cuban Revolution is not a matter of solidarity nor, to say the least, a profitable commercial venture. As with everything else we publish, our purpose is to produce the works that revolutionary-minded workers, farmers, and young people within the United States need in order to be more effective. And the Cuban Revolution is today the only example in the world of a communist leadership that has taken and holds state power and uses that most important of all levers to advance the world struggle for socialism, both inside Cuba and internationally. A leadership that fights to lead the working class along its line of march, not to stifle or oppose it.

Pathfinder's publishing of pamphlets and books about

the Cuban Revolution began within the first months of the revolutionary victory in 1959. Among the earliest pamphlets were the speech on the first agrarian reform and "The Revolution Must Be a School of Unfettered Thought," both by Fidel Castro. Another was the pamphlet prepared by *Militant* reporter Harry Ring in 1961, based on his visits to Cuba, entitled *How Cuba Uprooted Race Discrimination*. It is a wonderful pamphlet, reprinted from the pages of the *Militant*, of course. I remember what a powerful impact it had on me when I first came around the communist movement about that time—just as the mass street battles to bring down the Jim Crow system of segregation in the United States were gaining such momentum. It helped recruit me.

One of the most effective titles we have published in recent years is a collection entitled *To Speak the Truth*. It includes the three speeches given over the years by Fidel and by Che before the United Nations General Assembly—in 1960, 1964, and 1979—plus the speech by Che in 1964 to the Geneva conference on trade sponsored by the United Nations. We subtitled that collection, "Why Washington's 'Cold War' Against Cuba Doesn't End," because more than any other book we have, Fidel's and Che's speeches before the United Nations explain the origins of the U.S. rulers' war against the Cuban Revolution and why they will never forgive the working people of Cuba for charting their own independent course.

All these books have been sold in thousands of copies across the U.S. from street tables as well as through big commercial bookstores and chains. They have been used in classes and study circles in dozens of cities and towns. They have been carried into factories, mills, and mines in lunch buckets and coat pockets to be shown to interested co-workers.

'Communist Manifesto' is top seller

I think that perhaps the best way to capture many things about the class struggle in the United States today, and the opportunities that exist for communists, is to tell you what the best-selling titles produced by Pathfinder are. Our number one best-seller year after year is the *Communist Manifesto.* Second are books by Malcolm X. And third are books by Che Guevara.

That hit parade says a lot!

I could add that last year—1997—our two best-sellers were the *Communist Manifesto* and *Pombo: A Man of Che's 'guerrilla.'* And among our top fifteen titles, six were related to the Cuban Revolution—including the *Bolivian Diary, Che Guevara Speaks, Episodes of the Cuban Revolutionary War,* and the pamphlet of interviews with Gen. Harry Villegas, *At the Side of Che Guevara.* Six others were collections of speeches by Malcolm X or other titles related to the Black struggle in the U.S. Two were basic texts of the modern communist movement—the *Communist Manifesto* and *Socialism: Utopian and Scientific.* And the remaining title in the top fifteen was *The Truth about Yugoslavia: Why Working People Should Oppose Intervention,* explaining the roots of the current war in that country and imperialism's interests there.

As a new war crisis confronts us in the Mideast, that lineup will shift somewhat in 1998. I dare to predict that *U.S.*

Hands Off the Mideast! will once again move toward the ranks of the best-sellers, and the example of the Cuban Revolution will come into sharp relief from a slightly different direction.

Once again, it will be the opportunity for men and women within the United States who unflinchingly oppose the war drive of Washington and its allies to help produce and expand and sell in increasing numbers the arsenal of political weapons that working people the world over need—publications that tell the truth about imperialism and war, and why the interests of working people the world over are irreconcilable with those of the exploiting classes.

Of one thing we can be sure. The demand for such books will grow.

BUILDING A PROLETARIAN PARTY

The Low Point of Labor Resistance Is Behind Us

The Socialist Workers Party Looks Forward

JACK BARNES
MARY-ALICE WATERS
STEVE CLARK

The global order imposed by Washington after its victory in World War II is shattering. A long retreat by the working class and unions has come to an end. The bosses and their government are stepping up attacks on our wages, conditions, and constitutional rights. This book highlights opportunities for building a mass proletarian party able to lead the struggle to end capitalist rule, opening a socialist future for humanity. $10. Also in Spanish and French.

Labor, Nature, and the Evolution of Humanity

The Long View of History

FREDERICK ENGELS, KARL MARX
GEORGE NOVACK, MARY-ALICE WATERS

Without understanding that social labor, transforming nature, has driven humanity's evolution for millions of years, working people are unable to see beyond the capitalist epoch of class exploitation that warps all human relations, ideas, and values. Only the revolutionary conquest of state power by the working class can open the door to a world free of capitalist exploitation, degradation of nature, subjugation of women, racism, and war. A world built on human solidarity. A socialist world. $12. Also in Spanish and French.

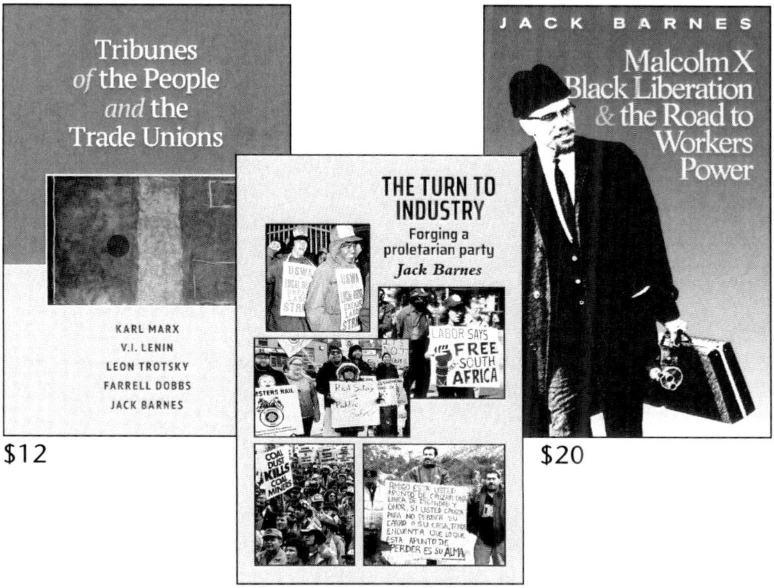

$12

$20

$15

Three books to be read as one . . .

about building a party that's working class in program, composition, and action. One that recognizes, in word and deed, the most revolutionary fact of our time . . .

. . . that working people have the power to create a different world as we act together to defend our own class interests—not those of the privileged classes who exploit our labor, not of those who fear us as "deplorables," or just plain "trash."

As we advance along a revolutionary course toward workers power, we will transform ourselves and awaken to our own worth. Also in Spanish, French, Greek.

Special Offer!
All three $30

The Turn to Industry and *Tribunes of the People and the Trade Unions* $20

Either book plus *Malcolm X, Black Liberation, and the Road to Workers Power* $25

PATHFINDERPRESS.COM

CAPITALIST CRISIS AND THE FIGHT FOR WORKERS POWER

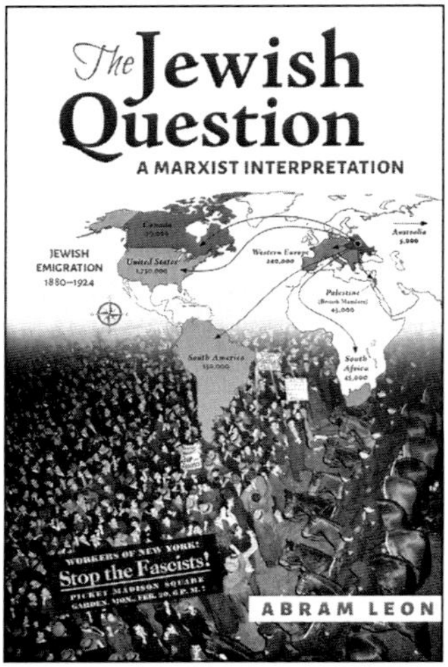

The Jewish Question

A Marxist Interpretation

ABRAM LEON

The battle against reactionary forces aiming to exterminate the Jews remains central to world politics, as shown by the genocidal October 2023 pogrom in Israel. Why is Jew-hatred still raising its ugly head? What are its class roots? Why, as Abram Leon explains, is there no solution "independent of the world proletarian revolution"? Revised translation, new introduction, and 40 pages of illustrations and maps. $17. Also in Spanish and French.

The Clintons' Anti-Working-Class Record

Why Washington Fears Working People

JACK BARNES

What working people need to know about the profit-driven course of Democrats and Republicans alike over the last three decades. And the political awakening of workers seeking to understand and resist the capitalist rulers' assaults. $10. Also in Spanish, French, Farsi, Greek.

Are They Rich Because They're Smart?

Class, Privilege, and Learning under Capitalism

JACK BARNES

Exposes growing class inequalities in the US and the self-serving rationalizations of well-paid professionals who think their "brilliance" equips them to "regulate" working people, who don't know what's in our own best interest. $10. Also in Spanish, French, Farsi, Arabic.

CUBA'S SOCIALIST REVOLUTION

New Edition!

Che Guevara on Economics and Politics in the Transition to Socialism

CARLOS TABLADA

It's essential for working people to win state power, said Ernesto Che Guevara. "Then there's the second stage, maybe more difficult than the first"—the transition from dog-eat-dog capitalism to socialism. That includes moving from work as a condition for survival, to voluntary social labor through which we express our common humanity. Includes Fidel Castro's 1987 speech "Che's Ideas are Absolutely Relevant Today." New edition with substantially expanded selections from Guevara's writings. $17. Also in Spanish, coming in French.

Cuba and the Coming American Revolution

JACK BARNES

This is a book about the example set by the Cuban people that socialist revolution is not only necessary—it can be made. A book about the struggles of workers and other exploited producers in the imperialist heartland, and the youth attracted to them. About the class struggle in the US, where the revolutionary capacities of working people are as utterly discounted by the ruling powers as were those of the Cuban toilers. And just as wrongly. $10. Also in Spanish, French, Farsi.

Women in Cuba: The Making of a Revolution within the Revolution

VILMA ESPÍN, ASELA DE LOS SANTOS, YOLANDA FERRER

The integration of women in the ranks and leadership of the Cuban Revolution was intertwined with the proletarian course of the leadership of the revolution from the start. This is the story of that revolution and how it transformed the women and men who made it. $17. Also in Spanish, Farsi, Greek.

EXPAND YOUR REVOLUTIONARY LIBRARY

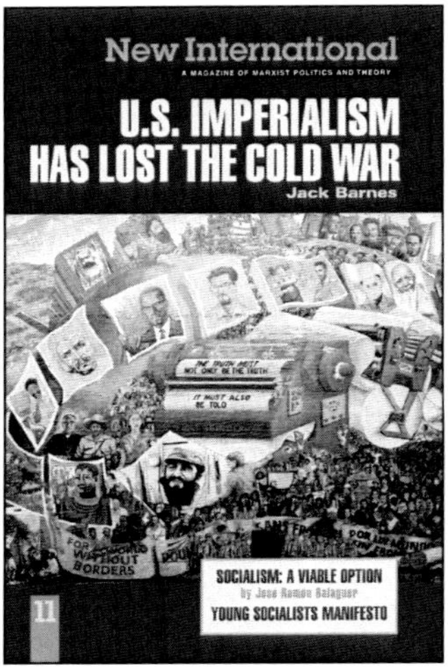

U.S. Imperialism Has Lost the Cold War

JACK BARNES

The collapse of regimes across Eastern Europe and the USSR claiming to be communist did not mean workers and farmers there had been crushed. In today's sharpening class conflicts and wars, these toilers are joining working people the world over in the class struggle against capitalist exploitation. In *New International* no. 11. $14. Also in Spanish, French, Farsi, Greek.

Opening Guns of World War III: Washington's Assault on Iraq

JACK BARNES

The murderous assault on Iraq in 1990–91 heralded increasingly sharp conflicts among imperialist powers, growing instability of capitalism, and more wars. Also includes:

1945: When US Troops Said No! by Mary-Alice Waters

Lessons from the Iran-Iraq War by Samad Sharif

In *New International* no. 7. $14. Also in Spanish, French, Farsi.

Cosmetics, Fashions, and the Exploitation of Women

JOSEPH HANSEN, EVELYN REED
MARY-ALICE WATERS

How big business reinforces women's second-class status and uses it to rake in profits. Where does women's oppression come from? How has the entry of millions of women into the workforce strengthened the battle for emancipation, still to be won? $12. Also in Spanish, Farsi, Greek.

Teamster Rebellion

FARRELL DOBBS

The 1934 strikes that won union recognition for truckers and warehouse workers in Minneapolis and helped pave the way for the working-class social movement that built the industrial unions. The first of four volumes by a central leader of these battles. $16. Also in Spanish, French, Farsi, Greek.

Lenin's Final Fight

Speeches and Writings, 1922–23

V.I. LENIN

In 1922 and 1923, V.I. Lenin, central leader of the world's first socialist revolution, waged what was to be his last political battle—one that was lost after his death. At stake was whether that revolution, and the international communist movement it led, would remain on the revolutionary proletarian course that brought workers and peasants to power in October 1917. $17. Also in Spanish, Farsi, Greek.

Pathfinder Press **accessible e-books** for the blind, those with low vision, or other challenges reading print books

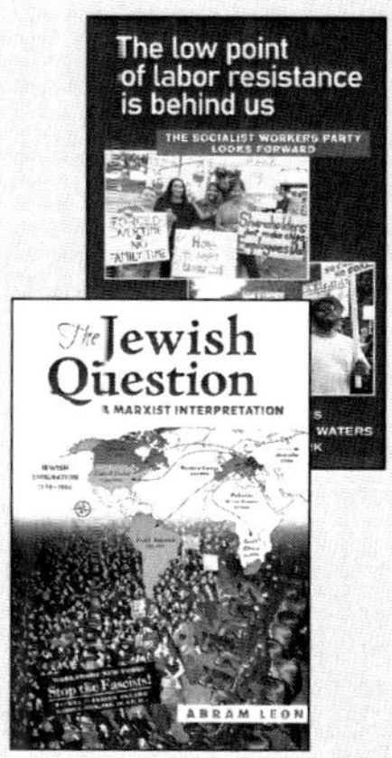

For a list of current accessible titles, go to: pathfinderpress.com/collections/books-for-the-blind.

Visit bookshare.org for information on how to sign up.